World Cultural and Natural Heritage
(China Volume)

The Mountain Resort and Outlying Temples

By Ji Jiuli

China Pictorial Publishing House

The above pattern is the mark of the *Convention for the Protection of World Cultural and Natural Heritage*. The shape of the square in the circle, which symbolizes nature, is created by the human race. The pattern, with the square and the circle linked together, implies the close relation between the cultural heritage and the natural heritage, and appeals to the human beings to protect the cultural and natural heritage in the world.

Front cover Autumn scenery of the Mountain Resort. By Chen Keyin
Back cover The Jinshan Islet. By Chen Baosen

This picture album is published in both Chinese and English.

Academic Consultants

Hou Renzhi	Academician of the Chinese Academy of Sciences, Professor of Peking University
Zheng Xiaoxie	Vice president of the Committee of Specialists of Preservation on Historical Cultural Cities &Towns, China
Luo Zhewen	Chairman of Society of Chinese Cultural Relics

By He Shiyao

Publisher's Words

For the purpose of protecting the world cultural and natural heritage, the UNESCO passed the *Convention for the Protection of World Cultural and Natural Heritage* in Paris on November 16, 1972. China joined the convention in 1978.

With a long history and a vast territory, China has a great many cultural and natural relics, 21 of which have been included on the *World Heritage List* by the World Heritage Commission of the UNESCO. They are: the Great Wall, the Imperial Palace of the Ming and Qing Dynasties, the Mogao Caves, the Mausoleum of the First Qin Emperor and Terracotta Warriors, the Peking Man Site, the Mount Taishan, the Mount Huangshan, the Jiuzhaigou Valley Scenic and Historic Interest Area, the Huanglong Scenic and Historic Interest Area, the Wulingyuan Scenic and Historic Interest Area, the Mountain Resort and Outlying Temples, the Temple and Cemetery of Confucius and the Kong Family Mansion, the Potala Palace, the Ancient Building Complex in the Wudang Mountains, the Mount Emei and Leshan Giant Buddha, the Lushan National Park, the Old City of Lijiang, the Old City of Pingyao, the Classical Gardens in Suzhou, the Summer Palace and the Temple of Heaven.

This picture album attempts to help readers better understand China's cultural and natural relics, and to do its bit for the protection of the historical sites of the mankind.

World Cultural and Natural Heritage
(China Volume)

The Mountain Resort and Outlying Temples

Co-compiled by the State Cultural Relics Bureau of the People's Republic of China and Beijing Jingxin Cultural Development Co., Ltd.

Chief Editor: Ru Suichu
Editor of the Volume: Zhou Yi

China Pictorial Publishing House
1999

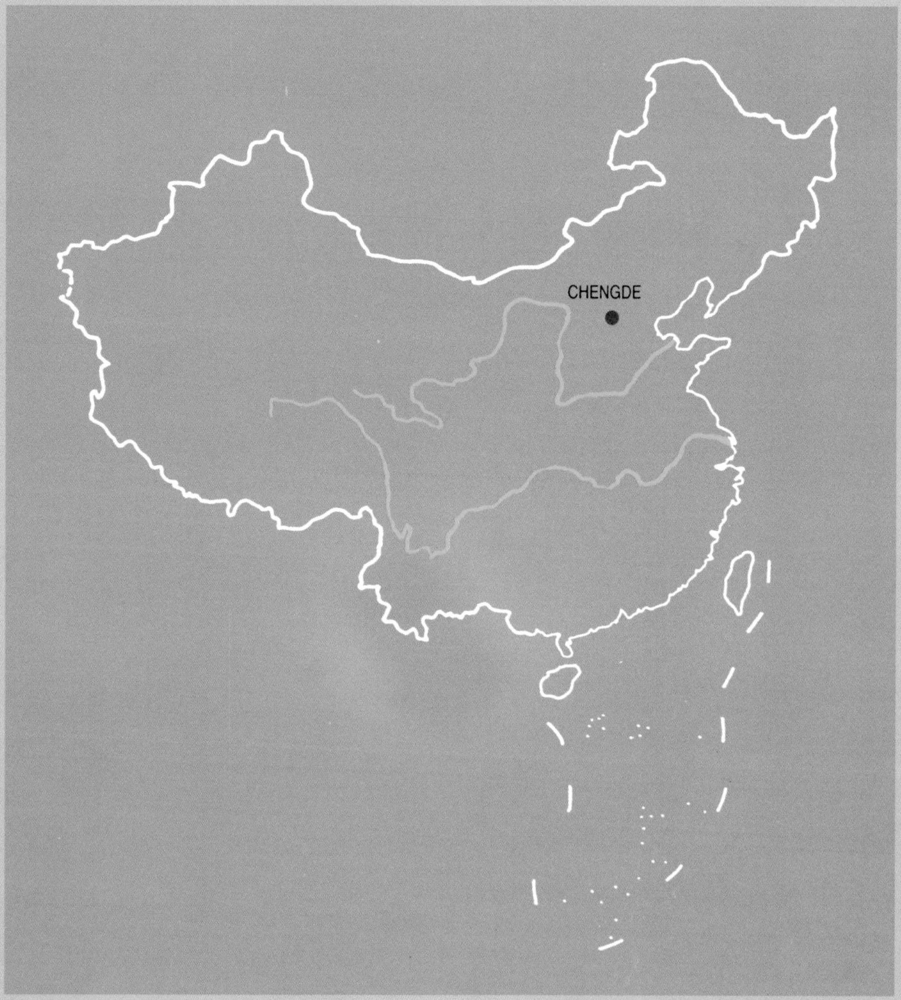

The Mountain Resort and Outlying Temples are located in Chengde City in northwest Hebei Province. The geographical coordinates are on the joint point of 118 degrees east longitude and 41 degrees north latitude. The location is in the transition area from the broadleaf forest of warm temperate zone to the grassland of temperate zone, with a cool, moderate and moist climate.

CONTENTS

1

1. The undulating hills of the Mountain Resort dimly visible in the mist after the rain. By Chen Keyin

2

2. Morning on the Zhijing Yundi, an enchanting scene similar in areas south of the Yangtze River. By Shi Ling

3

3. Pulesi with a unique architectural style.   By He Shiyao

4

4. Xumifushouzhimiao, an architectural complex of imposing grandeur. By Chen Baosen

5

5. Yongyousi, a regular lamasery in the plain area. By Chen Keyin

The Largest Existing Imperial Garden

- The Mountain Resort and Outlying Temples in Chengde are a treasure of ancient gardening arts still existing in China. They are the crystallization of the wisdom and labor of ancient Chinese garden architects, and are an important component of Chinese traditional culture.
- Emperor Kangxi had the Mountain Resort and Outlying Temples built in order to uphold the unification of the multi-national state and maintain the frontier stability. It used to be the No. 2 political center of the Qing Court.
- The 72 scenic spots with inscriptions by Emperor Kangxi and Emperor Qianlong are the essence of the Mountain Resort and Outlying Temples. This imperial garden assembles the beautiful sights common in areas south of the Yangtze River, on the grassland north of the Great Wall and on the plateau in northwest China. There are imitations of gardens in all parts of the country and magnificent temples in combined architectural styles of the Han, Mongolian and Tibetan nationalities as well.
- The Mountain Resort and Outlying Temples have been included on the *World Heritage List*, therefore, becoming the common wealth of human beings. The place is also a famous summer resort and scenic spot attracting tourists around the world.

The Mountain Resort and Outlying Temples in Chengde

By Du Jiang

The Largest Existing Imperial Garden

The Mountain Resort is located in Chengde City, north of Hebei Province and 250 km from Beijing. It was first built during the reign of Emperor Kangxi and has a history of nearly 300 years. Covering some 564 ha, it is the largest imperial garden existing in China today. There are a group of temples and monasteries surrounding the Mountain Resort, which have diversified architectural styles. In Chinese history, the construction of imperial gardens demonstrates from one aspect the achievements of ancient culture, art, science and technology, and is an important component of the Chinese traditional culture. Owing to historical reasons, many famous royal gardens built before the Ming and Qing dynasties no longer exist, which makes the Mountain Resort even more precious and an existing treasure of ancient gardening art. In 1994, the Mountain Resort and Outlying Temples were appraised by the World Heritage Commission of the UNESCO to be included on the *World Heritage List* and become the common wealth of human beings.

The location of Chengde lies in the transitional area between the Mongolian Plateau and the North China Plain, with a warm continental climate. The Saihanba in south of the Mongolian Plateau, like a natural defense, prevents the incursion of the cold currents from Siberia and forms a regional small climate with a temperate climate, abundant rainfall and luxuriant plants. The annual average temperature in the city is 8.9℃, with the highest 24.4℃ in summer. With no sweltering hot weather, it is indeed a summer resort.

The Mountain Resort, also known as Jehol Imperial Palace or Chengde Temporary Abode for the Emperor, was first built in the 42nd year during the reign of Emperor Kangxi (1703). It took nearly 90 years to complete the construction in the 57th year during the reign of Emperor Qianlong (1792). The two emperors each named 36 scenic spots of the resort. Emperor Kangxi even wrote a poem, describing the scenery as "Fish jumps on the waves when spring comes, geese rest on the sand when autumn falls, everywhere there are fairy plants, and by the window are greeting flowers." He compared the resort with the beautiful sights in areas south of the Yangtze River, with the former unique with its simple and rustic scenery.

6

6. A panoramic view of the Mountain Resort. By Chen Keyin

7

8

7. A picture drawn by Leng Mei (Qing) of the 36 scenic spots named by Emperor Kangxi.
Courtesy of Luo Zhewen

8. A general view of the Mountain Resort.
Courtesy of Chen Keyin

The Mountain Resort has four parts according to the natural condition: the palace area, the lake area, the plain area and the mountain area. The palace area lies in the south of the resort, and used to be the place for grand ceremonies, the emperor to handle court affairs and the living quarters of the imperial family. In the southeast of the resort sits the lake area . With lush southern-type fields in this place north of the Great Wall, there are lakes dotted with islets and waters merging with the limitless sky, a touch of the entire layout of the resort. In the north is the plain area where there are towering old trees and boundless grasslands. In the northwest are forested mountains with deep gullies, rising and falling ridges, and temples and buildings hidden amidst pines and cypresses. Among the rocks, streams and plants, more than 120 architectural complexes were built, copies from famous landscaped gardens in other parts of China such as the Lion Grove in Suzhou, Jinshan Temple in Zhenjiang, Tower of Mist and Rain in Jiaxing, and Tianyige Chamber in Ningbo. This well reflects the intention of the emperor to include all beauties and wonders on earth in his palm. Emperor Kangxi named 36 scenic spots in the resort with four Chinese characters. His grandson, Emperor Qianlong, followed suit later and named another 36 scenic spots with three Chinese characters.

The outlying temples are scattered in the north and east of the resort, just like a myriad of stars surrounding the moon. Most of them are lamaseries and the emperor had them built to unite the Mongolian, Tibetan and other frontier ethnic groups, and safeguard the unification and stability of the country, so as to strengthen the northern frontier and defend the invasion of Russia. In respect to architecture, these temples combine the essence of the building arts of the Han, Mongolian and Tibetan nationalities. During the 67 years from the 52nd year in the reign of Emperor Kangxi (1713) to the 45th year in the reign of Emperor Qianlong (1780), 12 temples were built. Eight of them were lamaseries under the administration of the Lifanyuan (Superintendency of Dependencies). Since they were located north of the Great Wall at Gubcikou, hence the name "kouwai bamiao" or "eight outlying temples". These temples look resplendent and magnificent with gorgeous colors, a sharp contrast with the simple architectural style of

the resort.

The Mountain Resort and Outlying Temples, which assemble various scenes in areas south of the Yangtze River, on the grasslands beyond the Great Wall and on the northwest plateau within one garden enclosed by a 10-km wall, together with the temples with diversified architectural styles of different nationalities, could be seen as a miniature of the vast Chinese territory. It was right in here, a symbolic environment of the unification of the country, that the Qing emperors handled national affairs.

Although the country was united in early Qing Dynasty, various elements of turbulence still existed during the reign of Emperor Kangxi, for instance, the revolt of the three feudatories headed by Wu Sangui in the 12th year (1673), the rebellion of the Mongolian Chahar tribe in the 14th year (1675), the separatist rule of a Mongolian tribe in the west, and the aggression of Russia in the north. To safeguard the northern frontier, Emperor Kangxi, a man of great talent and bold strategy, decided an imperial hunting ground to be built in a place with convenient transportation to various Mongolian tribes. It was called Mulan Weichang or Mulan Imperial Hunting Ground, in today's Weichang Manchu and Mongolia Autonomous County some 150 km north of Chengde. With the establishment of the hunting ground, military training and defense preparations were reinforced, and good relationship with the Mongolian nobility was strengthened. From the 22nd year during the reign of Emperor Kangxi (1683) , an annual autumn hunting activity, known as "Mulan Qiuxian", with the participation of 12,000 soldiers was held in the Mulan Imperial Hunting Ground. It was a large-scale hunting and military maneuver. The building of the Mountain Resort was closely related with such a special historical background.. As early as in 1677 when Emperor Kangxi made an inspection tour to the north, he had an imperial palace built in Kalahetun (today's Xiluanhe Town, Chengde), the first temporary dwelling place for the emperor built north of the Great Wall at Gubeikou. The emperor himself had received the heads of the Mongolian tribes here. After the Mulan Imperial Hunting Ground was set up, the emperor led his troops on hunting there almost every autumn and received the heads of

9

10

Mongolian tribes and frontier ethnic groups. However, the narrow region of Kalahetun and the short stay at Mulan of the emperor limited the implementation of safeguarding the frontier stability and the policies toward the Mongolians. It became urgent to build a larger imperial palace at a proper place.

In winter of 1701, Emperor Kangxi set off his hunting north of the Great Wall at Xifengkou and looking for an ideal place for the new imperial palace. When he visited Shangying at Jehol (the location of today's Mountain Resort), he looked around at the surrounding mountains, winding clean streams, and row upon row of peculiar peaks and queer rocks, and said with emotion that the place was gifted with the majesty of mountains in northwest China and the seclusion of mountains in the southeast, which had both been praised by ancient people. Concerning the strategic importance, it could command the vast Mongolian desert in the north and guard the capital of Beijing in the south. Besides, the place had not been inhabited for a long time and thus the possible disturbance of the civilians and requisition of the arable land could both be avoided. The location was quite near to Beijing and the Mulan Imperial Hunting Ground, and the memorials to the emperor sent in the morning could arrive in the evening, making no difference with the imperial palace in the capital city. Thinking of this, the emperor ordered an imperial palace be built right here.

The Mountain Resort in Chengde had not only been a mountain hamlet for the Qing emperors to escape the heat, but also a place for them to handle the state political and military affairs, with national affairs in particular. The Qing emperors strengthened their relations with the princes, dukes and nobility of the minority nationalities by means of offering official posts, granting rewards, having audiences, hunting, recital ceremony and scripture chanting, thus safeguarding the unification of the Qing court and the unity of the nationalities.

From the building of the Jehol Imperial Palace to the completion of the Mountain Resort, the place became the summer resort for the Qing emperors on progresses and a provisional capital. Especially during the reign of Emperor Kangxi and Emperor Qianlong, they spent half of the year in Chengde. Consequently, a series of service organs and facilities were needed to be built, such as palaces for the princes, government offices, post-houses, schools, teahouses, restaurants and wine shops. During the late years of Emperor Kangxi, Chengde had grown into a prosperous town.

Making a general survey of the history of the Qing Dynasty, the Mountain Resort witnessed the thriving and declining of the Qing court from a unique angle. It was in its prime during the prosperity time under the reign of Emperor Kangxi and Emperor Qianlong. However, along with the gradual declining of the Qing court in the late years of Emperor Qianlong, the Mountain Resort became on the wane. Emperor Jiaqing only occasionally went to Chengde to escape the summer heat or hunt in the Mulan Imperial Hunting Ground since the ancestral instruction chould not be defied. In the fourth year of the reign of Emperor Daoguang (1824), the traditional rite of autumn hunting was abolished and the emperor no longer inspected the areas north of the Great Wall or hunted at Mulan in autumn.

In late Qing Dynasty, the ancient buildings and gardens of the Mountain Resort and Outlying Temples were left in a state of collapse, destruction or erosion by wind and rain.

In the decades after the downfall of the Qing Dynasty, the Mountain Resort and Outlying Temples even became devastated with destruction by man.

After the People's Republic of China was founded in 1949, large-scale renovation has been made to the Mountain Resort and Outlying Temples, restoring the original appearance. In 1961, some of the temples were included on the list of the first group of cultural relics under state protection, which was released by the State Council. Later, it was selected one of the 10 national scenic spots and became a famous place of interest attracting tourist at home and abroad.

11

9. A portrait of Emperor Kangxi.
Courtesy of Ge Honghui
10. A portrait of Emperor Qianlong.
Courtesy of Ge Honghui
11. A picture of hunting.
Courtesy of Chen Keyin

A sketch map of the Mountain Resort and Outlying Temples.

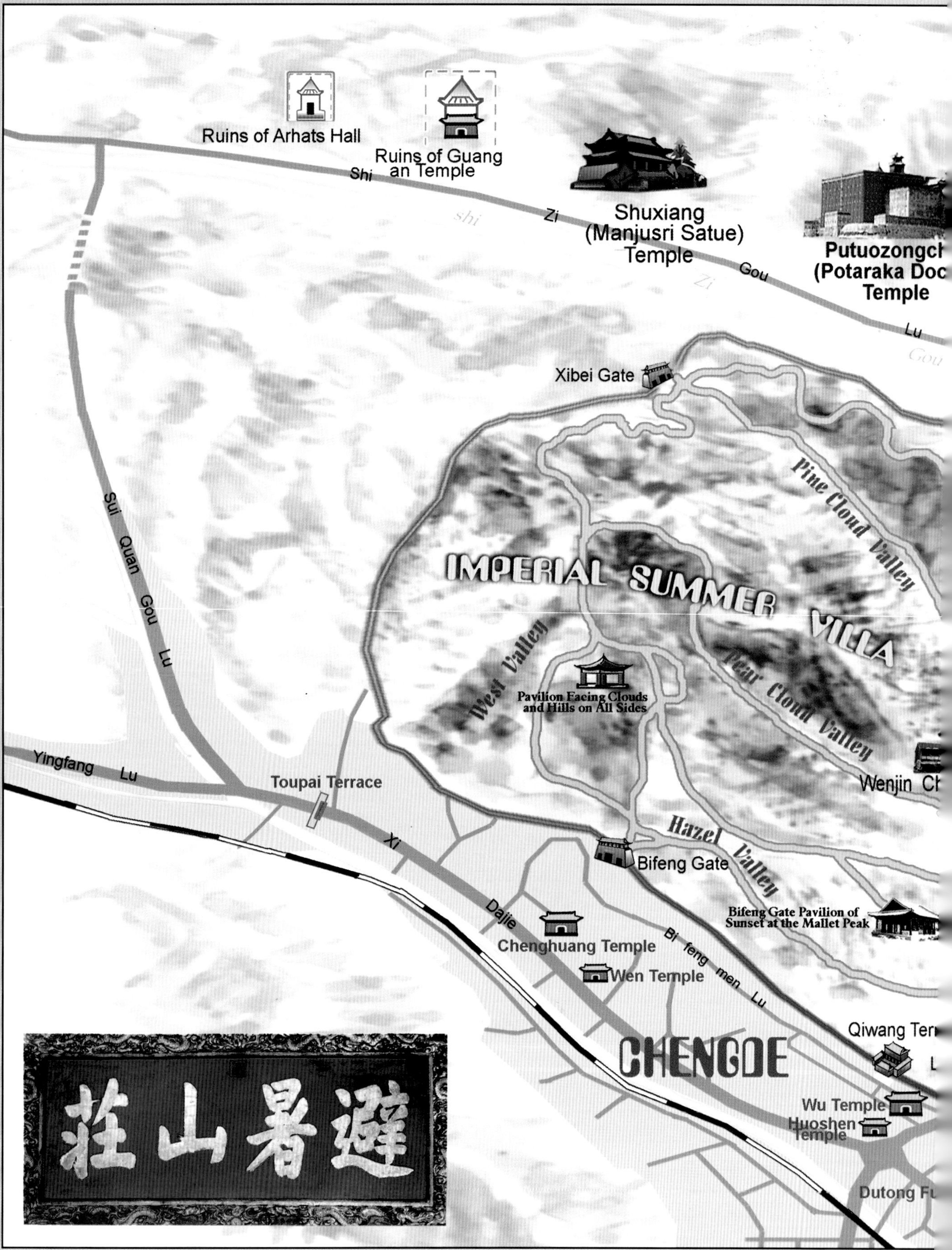

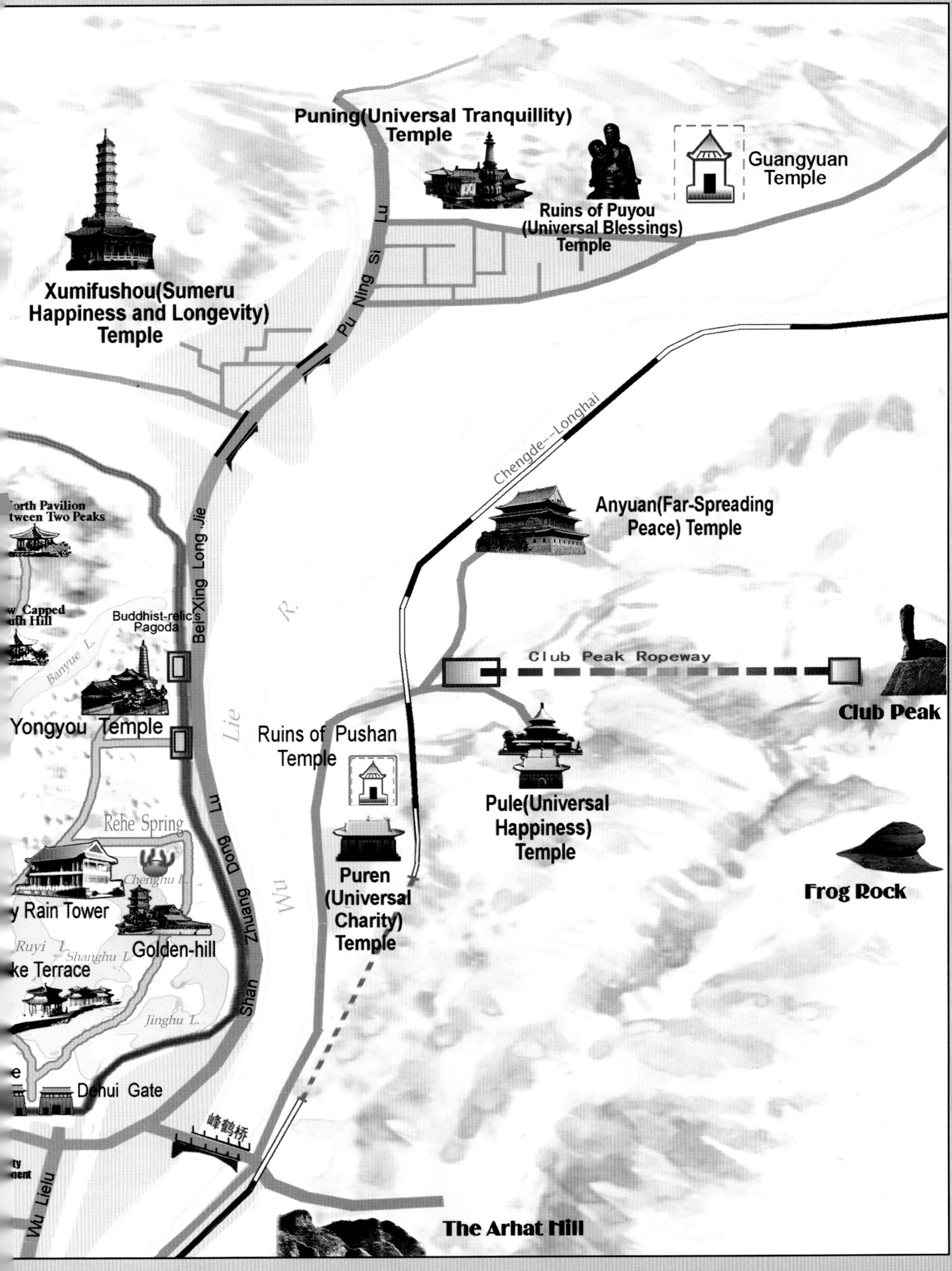

Authar:Wu Xiaogan

12

12. Summer on the Jinshan Islet.   By Chen Keyin

Splendors of the Mountain Resort

- The Mountain Resort has four parts: the palace area, the lake area, the plain area and the mountain area. There are solemn palaces, picturesque scenes common in areas south of the Yangtze River, scenery with rustic charms on boundless grassland, and rising and falling mountain ridges.
- The lake area is dotted with islets, with the water and the sky blended in one color. Eight lakes of different shapes form a sight of seclusion with winding banks and delicate bridges, which earn the place fame of "lush southern-type fields north of the Great Wall".
- The plain area boasts fertile land and luxuriant forests and plants. There used to be large yurts and yellow tents especially for the emperors. Emperor Qianlong once received religious and national heads and foreign envoys here.
- The mountain area has rising and falling mountain ridges, crisscross valleys and ravines and dense forests, among which hide gardens, temples and pavilions. This part could be said the cream of the Mountain Resort. Ascending a height, tourists can enjoy a distant view of the entire resort.

13

Splendors of the Mountain Resort

The layout and style of the resort are different from common landscape gardens. It has both solemn palaces, pastoral scenes in areas south of the Yangtze River, scenery on boundless grassland, and rising and falling mountain ridges. It embraces both the beautiful scenery of lakes and mountains similar to the West Lake in Hangzhou, and the quiet seclusion well-known of gardens in Suzhou. As a grand imperial garden, the resort makes a harmonious combination of the delicacy of the south and the majesty of the north within one garden, embodying the idea of "containing the heaven and the earth within one heart" by the emperor when building the garden.

I. Palace Area

The palace area is where the emperor dealt with state affairs and where the empress and the concubines lived. Located in the southeast of the resort, this area is right on a platform between the mountain area and the lake area. It consists of four palaces of Zhenggong (Front Palace), Songhezhai (Pine-Crane Hall), Wanhe Songfeng (Pine Soughing Valleys) and Donggong (East Palace). Different from the Imperial Palace in Beijing, these palaces are in the style of civil residences in north China, all built with gray bricks and tiles instead of colored glaze, and no color paintings on the beams and columns. Therefore, they don't look as magnificent as the Imperial Palace in Beijing. They were built on the order of the emperor to highlight the theme of "resort" with rustic mountainous charms. Only living in such a place could the emperor forget the "mundane life".

Danbo Jingcheng Dian (Hall of Simplicity and Sincerity)
It is the main hall of the Front Palace where ceremonies were held and the emperors gave audiences. Surrounded by verdant old pines, the environment is tranquil and solemn. Since the hall was built all with *nanmu*, it got the name of Nanmu Hall. The 48 hardwood *nanmu* pillars give off a delicate scent, which makes people refreshing upon entering the hall. Inscribed on

14

the horizontal board hung in the hall are four Chinese characters "Danbo Jingcheng" by Emperor Kangxi. They were taken from *Jiezi Shu,* or *Letter of Cautions to the Descendants*, by Zhuge Liang, "show high ideals by simple living and accomplish something lasting by leading a quiet life". The emperor chose it as self-examination and to restrain his descendants.

Sizhi Shuwu (Four Knowledge Study) It used to be a place for the emperor to call in officials to discuss state affairs and receive important leaders of the minority nationalities. The inscription of the study was written by Emperor Qianlong. In the middle of the board was stamped a seal of the emperor, saying "wufu wudai guxi tianzi zhibao", indicating it was the seal of Emperor Qianlong who was by then in his 70s (called *guxi* in Chinese) and had five generations in his royal family. The phrase "sizhi" (four knowledge) comes from *Yijing*, or *The Book of Changes*, an ancient Chinese classics. A gentleman is one who knows what is soft, strong, small and obvious before he becomes the hope of all things on earth. Emperor Qianlong knew well that an emperor should learn to handle state affairs with both mailed fist and velvet glove, and a combined use of overt and covert means so as to maintain a lasting political stability of the country.

13. Danbo Jingcheng Dian was the main hall of the Front Palace where significant ceremonies were held, or the emperor received important envoys during his stay in the Mountain Resort. By Chen Keyin
14. Sizhi Shuwu was the place where the emperor called in officials to discuss state affairs and gave audiences to minority prices and nobility. By Ji Zeng

15

Yanbo Zhishuang Dian (Hall of Refreshing Mists and Waves)
It was the bedchamber of the Qing emperors. Emperors Kangxi, Qianlong, Jiaqing and Xianfeng had lived here.

Yunshan Shengdi Lou (Viewing Misty Mountain Tower)
Behind the Yanbo Zhishuang Dian is a two-story five-bay-wide building. There is a lotus room upstairs where the *Huayan Scripture* and a jade Buddha are enshrined. Downstairs is a small indoor stage to present opera performances for the emperor and his royal family. The tower has no real stairs, but rockeries are cleverly used instead. Ascending the tower, people can have a panoramic view of the lakes and mountains of the resort.

Wanhe Songfeng (Pine Soughing Valleys)
Lying to the east of the Front Palace, it perches beyond a lake and hidden in the green of pine forest. Emperor Kangxi often read over memorials and received officials here. In the 61st

16

year of his reign (1722), he had 12-year-old Hongli (later Emperor Qianlong) living in the imperial palace. He liked Hongli so much that Hongli accompanied him when he made inspections out of the capital or hunted in the Mulan Imperial Hunting Ground. During his stay in the Mountain Resort, he had a study built to the south of Wanhe Songfeng especially for Hongli so that he could give him instructions every day. When Emperor Kangxi gave audiences to officials, he often let his grandson stay to learn imperial ceremony and propriety. After Emperor Qianlong succeeded to the throne, he changed the name of the main hall to Jientang (Hall of Gratitude).

Juane Shengjing Dian (Hall of Juane Splendors)

It is an ideal place for banquet. The allusion of "Juane Shengjing" comes from an ancient legend. When Chengwang of the Zhou Dynasty was still young, Zhou Gongdan assisted him in governing the country. One day when Chengwang went on sight-seeing in Mount Qishan with the companion of officials, there was gentle breeze from the winding cols. Zhou wrote *Juane Fu*, in which he likened the breeze to the harmonious relationship between the king and his officials and exhorted Chengwang to appoint virtuous and talented people. Standing in front the hall, people can enjoy the beautiful scene of the mountains in the north, which is quite similar to the Mount Qishan and Mount Juaneshan in Shaanxi Province. That Emperor Qianlong had the Juane Shengjing Dian built indicated his self-appraisal of his august wisdom.

17

15. Yanbo Zhishuang Dian was the bedchamber of the emperor where his empress and concubines made obeisance to him. With a simple and elegant appearance, the hall is magnificent with sumptuous interior furnishing. By Chen Keyin
16. Wanhe Songfeng was where Emperor Kangxi read books or read over memorials, and received officials. The building, standing on a hillock and looking out on a lake, has a clever layout and unique architectural style. By Chen Baosen
17. Shuifang Yanxiu on the Ruyizhou used to be a place for the empress dowager, the empress and the concubines to beg for cleverness on the 7th evening of the 7th lunar month. By Chen Keyin

18

II. Lake Area

The lake area is an important part of the Mountain Resort. Lying to the north of the palace area, it occupies about 14% of the total area of the resort. Of the 72 scenic spots named by Emperor Kangxi and Emperor Qianlong, 31 are scattered in the lake area. Both the emperors had inspected the areas south of the Yangtze River six times in their lives. They had the beautiful gardens in south China drawn and copied those excellent ones in the resort according to the conditions. Take the lake area for example. The lakes are divided into eight parts with dikes imitating the Su Dike and Bai Dike in the West Lake in Hangzhou. Thus, there are winding banks, dotted islets and bridges, forming a scene of quiet seclusion. Miniature scenic spots are built on the islets and sand bars to create an effect as described in a poem: "Mountains multiply, streams double back—I doubt there's even a road; Willows cluster darkly, blossoms shine—another village ahead!" With no artificial piling of bricks or stones, the banks look quite natural. The willow branches sway gently in the breeze, the breeze ripples the surface of the lake, and the calamus and lotus give off faint scent in the air, adding more charms to the lake.

Shuixinxie (Mid-Lake Pavilions) Sitting on the eight-gate stone sluice are three pavilions with a rectangular one in the middle and two square ones on the ends. The drop between the Yinhu Lake and the Xiahu Lake makes the water flow day and night with a beautiful waterfall. In hot summer, cool breeze blows with lotus fragrance, quite refreshing on the Shuixinxie.

Wenyuan (Lion Grove) Facing the Shuixinxie across the lake, Wenyuan was built in the 40th year of the reign of Emperor Qianlong (1775). Modeled on the Lion Grove in Suzhou, Wenyuan has rockeries arranged like clouds, hence the fame of "kingdom of rockeries". Among the rockeries are dotted 16 scenic spots, which are accessible by way of small bridges and stone steps, thus forming a miniature garden within the resort.

Jinshan (Golden Hill) On an islet with a forest of rockeries on east Chenghu Lake, a group of structures were modeled on the Jinshan Temple in Zhenjiang, Jiangsu Province. On the west bank is a dock. Ascending the stairs is the Shangdige (Tower of God) where the Jade Emperor and the Zhenwu Emperor are enshrined.

Rehequan (Jehol Spring) One of the major water sources in the resort, clear water bubbles like strings of pearls out of the Jehol Spring. In late autumn when cold air falls, vapors rise from the Jehol Spring because of the higher temperature of the water, thus forming one of the pleasant sights in the resort.

19

20

18. Shuixinxie, three pavilions on the stone sluice, is a unique scene in the resort. By Chen Shuhua
19. Yanyulou on the Qingliandao used to be a place Emperor Qianlong often visited to enjoy the view in the rain. By Shi Yi

20. Canglangyu with delicate buildings is a mini-garden on the Ruyizhou. By Chen Keyin
21. Yuese Jiangsheng is a quiet place except the sound of waves beating the lake banks under the bright moonlight. By Yun Long

21

22

23

Zhijing Yundi (Zigzag Path and Cloudy Dike) It is a copy of the Su Dike in the West Lake of Hangzhou. The dike links three islets in shapes of flower (Huanbi), cloud (Yuese Jiangsheng) and *ruyi* (Ruyizhou). Walking on the dike, people may feel like being in areas south of the Yangtze River with the bright ripples spreading on the lakes on both sides, green swaying willow branches and fragrant lotus flowers. The scene may remind tourists of Spring on the Su Dike, one of the 10 famous sights of the West Lake.

Huanbi (Surrounded by Green Waters) It is an islet in the shape of a flower. Surrounded by green waters on all sides, it gets its name. It used to be a place where the young princes studied while accompanying the emperor in the resort. On the north bank is a cottage pavilion in the shape of a bamboo hat with no color painting or decoration. Sometimes, royal concubines went boating or collecting water chestnuts and had a short rest here.

Yuese Jiangsheng (Moonlight and Gurgling Water) It is an islet in the shape of cloud. There is a four-courtyard compound with pines and rockeries. Emperor Kangxi and Emperor Qianlong often came to read in this quiet place or relieve summer heat here.

Ruyizhou (Good Luck Island) The biggest of the three islets, it gets its name for its shape of *ruyi*, an S-shaped ornamental object usually made of jade and a symbol of good luck. Consisting of hall and temple within a courtyard, it is an attraction combining the architectural styles typical in both north and south China.

Canglangyu (Surging Wave Islet) A garden on the Ruyizhou, it has rockeries and waterfalls which fall down into a pool. The opposite is a wide hall under the eaves of which hangs a board with the inscription of "Canglangyu" by Emperor Kangxi.

Yanyulou (Tower of Mist and Rain) Located on the Qingliandao (Green Lotus Islet) north of the Ruyizhou, it is a two-story building five bays wide. It was built after the Yanyulou in the South Lake in Jiaxing, Zhejiang Province in the 46th year during the reign of Emperor Qianlong (1781). It served as study of the emperor. Emperor Qianlong loved the tower very much and often came to view the surrounding scenery.

24

Fangyuanju (Fragrant Garden) Also called Business Street, it is a regular courtyard where the imperial porcelain, silk and jewelry were stored. A business street was opened in the courtyard for the empress and the concubines to look for fun and experience the life of common people. All vendors in the shops were acted by eunuchs.

Shuanghu Jiajing and Changhong Yinlian (Mirror of Two Lakes and Long Rainbow Lying Over the Water) Tothe north of the Fangyuanju is a stone bridge, which looks like a long rainbow lying over the rippling lakes. One memorial archway stands on each of the south and north ends of the bridge, with the inscriptions of "Changhong Yinlian" and "Shuanghu Jiajing" for each, both written by Emperor Kangxi. Aohan lotus are planted south of the bridge. When all other lotus flowers have withered, the Aohan lotus still bloom against the frost in autumn.

22. Rehequan in the northeast of the resort boasts warm spring water and is ice-free in winter. On the rock by the spring is inscribed the characters "Rehe" (Jehol). By Ji Jiuli
23. Wenyuan is famous for its rockeries with 16 scenic spots buried among them with compact layout. By Li Wenquan
24. Ascending the Shangdige on the Jinshan Islet, tourists can have a view of the mountains and the temples mirrored on the rippling lakes that are dotted with pleasure boats. By Chen Keyin

26

25. Jinshan Islet, which neighbors lakes on three sides and a stream on the fourth, boasts rockeries in various images and buildings scattered among them. By Chen Baosen
26. Shangdige on top of the Jinshan Peak is the highest spot in the lake area, where tourists can have a panoramic view of the lakes and the mountains. By Yang Bingqin
27. Shuiliu Yunzai is a square pavilion with verandahs on all sides and a total of 16 angles, hence the name, 16-angle pavilion. By Chen Baosen
28. Fangyuanju is the largest imperial storehouse in the resort. Various shops were built imitating the business street in the Yuanmingyuan in Beijing, where the empress and the concubines could have fun like on folk markets. By Chen Baosen

27

28

29

30

31

29. On the Huanbi Islet are a group of courtya
where the Buddhist Ghost Festival was h
on the 15th of the 7th lunar month. By th
decorated tents were set up, Buddhist bo
were made and lanterns lit, a quite liv
scene in the resort. By Ji Ze
30. When both red and white lotuses are in
bloom, the fragrance assails people's nos
By Hua Zhongm
31. In the spring in front of the Pingxiangp
grows aquatic plants in winter and duckwe
in summer, which give delicate scent agai

32

the heat. By Chen Baosen

32. Zhijing Yundi was piled up with the earth dug to make the lakes, similar as the making of the Su Dike in the West Lake. Walking on the dike in the rain mist, people may feel like in south China. By Yi Zhijian
33. Wenjinge, one of the four Qing imperial libraries, houses the Complete Collection in Four Treasuries and the Collection of Ancient and Contemporary Books. By Ji Jiuli

33

34

III. Plain Area

Occupying nearly 1,000 *mu* of grasslands, the plain area of the Mountain Resort is made up of two parts—the Wanshuyuan and the Shimadi. It's really an enchanting place with a carpet of luxuriant grass, colorful flowers dotted everywhere, herds of carefree Bavid's deer looking for food, hares running in the forests and pheasants flying out of the plants. There used to be large yurts and yellow tents built for the emperor. The surroundings were arranged in accordance with the customs and habits of the Mongolian people. Standing on the grasslands, tourists may have a special feeling as described in a folk song: "The sky is blue, blue; And the steppe wide, wide; Over grass that the wind has battered low, Sheep and oxen roam".

Wanshuyuan (10,000-Tree Garden) Covering some 870 *mu* of land in northeast of the plain area, it faces the Chenghu Lake in the south with mountains behind in the north. To keep the natural conditions here, few artificial structures were built when constructing the garden. Only 28 yurts were set up, with the largest 24 m in diameter, which was reserved for the emperor. It was in here that Emperor Qianlong once received the three leaders of the Mongolian Derbet tribe, head of the Torguts who returned to the motherland from the Volga River Valley and the sixth Panchen Lama. In 1793, the British envoy Macartney was also received by the emperor here.

Yongyousi Stupa It was modeled on the Liuheta Pagoda by the Qiantang River in Hangzhou and the Baoensi Pagoda in Nanjing. The octagonal stupa is 67 m high with nine stories. It looks magnificent with a gilded ball on top glittering under the sun. To the west is a tower where the portraits of the Qing emperors are enshrined. Every emperor who came to the resort had to, first of all, hold a memorial ceremony for all his ancestors here.

35

36

Wenjinge (Wenjin Chamber) One of the four imperial libraries of the Qing Dynasty, it was built after the Tianyige Chamber in Ningbo, Zhejiang Province. The chamber houses one set of the *Complete Collection in Four Treasuries* and the *Collection of Ancient and Contemporary Books* each. The *Complete Collection in Four Treasuries* was started to be compiled in the 38th year of the reign of Emperor Qianlong (1773) and it took more than 10 years to complete the project. The collection has four divisions of classics, history, philosophy and literature, hence, the name of "siku" or "four treasures". The 36,300-book encyclopedia includes 99,070 volumes in 3,457 categories, with some 774.93 million words. It is larger than both the *Yongle Dictionary* and the *Collection of Ancient and Contemporary Books*, and is the largest series of books in China and a rare collection in the world as well.

34. Wanshuyuan is a pasture with unique features of Mongolian grasslands. Large yurts and yellow tents had been built especially for the emperor. It used to be an important place for political activities during the reign of Emperor Qianlong. Courtesy of Chen Keyin

35. Emperor Qianlong receives the three leaders of the Mongolian Derbet tribe in the Wanshuyuan and bestowed banquet and conferred them titles of nobility. Courtesy of Chen Keyin

36. In 1793, the British envoy Macartney had an audience with Emperor Qianlong in the Wanshuyuan. Courtesy of Chen Keyin

37

38

39

37. On the carpet of luxuriant grass, there used to be herds of deer and today there are throngs of visitors. By Zhou Yi
38. On a tablet are inscribed one poem with five characters and one with seven characters to a line, both written by Emperor Qianlong. By Chen Keyin
39. Wanshuyuan, which used to be a place for political activities of Emperor Qianlong, now becomes a tourist holiday village. By Ji Zeng
40. Yongyousi Stupa in northeast of the Wanshuyuan was built to commemorate Emperor Qianlong's mother. By Chen Keyin

40

IV. Mountain Area

Mountains cover some four fifths of the total area of the Mountain Resort. The highest peak is 510 m above sea level, 180 m in elevation drop with the lake surface. Lying in the northwest of the resort, there are undulating mountains, crisscross valleys, luxuriant forests and murmuring streams around rocks, producing different scenery in four seasons of the year. More than 40 scenic spots had been built among the towering mountains and thick forests when Emperor Kangxi and Emperor Qianlong were in power. However, most of them had been destroyed, leaving ruins for later visitors to imagine their original elegance. In recent years, four reviewing pavilions have been renovated on top of four peaks. They are: Nanshan Jixue, Simian Yunshan, Beizhen Shuangfeng and Chuifeng Luozhao. Standing in any of them, people can have a panoramic view of the whole resort. Walking along the winding paths among forests, people may feel like entering Shangari-la with the purling streams, singing birds, delicate fragrance given off by flowers and plants. There are three valleys, each with a stoneslab-built imperial road leading to them.

Nanshan Jixue Ting (Pavilion Viewing Snow-Capped Mountains in the South) When spring is changing into summer, everywhere in the resort there is dense green, while ascending this pavilion, people can see snow still capping the mountains in the north like a jade screen, hence the name of the pavilion.

Qingfeng Luyu (Green Islet of Maple Trees) To the north of the Nanshan Jixue, there are a group of buildings buried among green maple grove. Seen from the Wanshuyuan, it looks like a green islet, hence the name. The maple trees are thick green in summer, while the frosty leaves are flaming in autumn.

Beizhen Shuangfeng Ting (Pavilion Viewing the Two Peaks in the North) Standing in the pavilion and looking into the distance in the north, people can see two peaks: one in the northwest and the other the northeast. They stand facing each other, like the two watchtowers on both sides of a palace gate.

41. In late autumn, the frosty maple is flaming on mountains in the south, quite dazzling to the eyes. By Chen Keyin
42. The winding palace wall surrounding the Mountain Resort looks like a miniature Great Wall, rising and falling with the mountain ridges and full of grandeur. By Chai Baozhong

42

41

43

Lihua Banyue (Pear Blossom Accompanying the Moon) There is a courtyard in the Lishuyu (Pear Tree Ravine). Backed with green mountains, it is a seclusive place. Particularly in spring, white pear blossom all over the mountains give off sweet smell, which is extremely enchanting under the bright moonlight.

Simian Yunshan Ting (Pavilion Viewing Clouds and Mountains) At the end of the Songlinyu (Pine Forest Ravine) and on the highest peak in the resort, perches a pavilion with the inscriptions by Emperor Kangxi. On the pillars inside are an antithetical couplet, saying "a high mountain gets the moonlight first, a lofty ridge enjoys the original wind naturally". The inspection of the emperor usually ended on the Double Ninth Festival (the 9th of the 9th lunar month) when the emperor would lead his officials and national heads ascending the pavilion and awarding them feasts of game. After the banquet, the national heads would return to their home and the emperor would leave for the capital.

Songhe Qingyue (Crane Singing Among the Pines) In the Zhenziyu (Hazel Ravine) is a courtyard by a stream, which bears an inscription by Emperor Kangxi. Amid fragrant grasses are exotic flowers and between old pine trees dance singing cranes. Emperor Kangxi had his mother living here to wish her a long life, because in Chinese, pine and crane are symbols of longevity.

Chuifeng Luozhao (Club Stone in the Setting Sun) On the north slope of the Songhe Qingyue is a shabby pavilion where Emperor Kangxi came to enjoying the view, especially the Club Stone in the setting sun.

Qiwanglou (Enchanting Viewing Tower) On the south slope of the Songhe Qingyue is a courtyard, which bears the inscription of Emperor Kangxi of "being open-hearted". Standing on the tower, people can have a marvelous view of the mountains and waters, the rosy dawn and evening mist, presenting a scene of boundless variety.

44

45

43. Beizhen Shuangfeng, which lies between the Jinshan Peak and the Heishan Peak, is one of the 36 scenic spots named by EmperorKangxi. By Chen Keyin
44. Nanshan Jixue glitters with white snow, presenting a magnificent northern scenery. By Shi Ling
45. To the north of the Songyunxia (Pine-Cloud Valley) perches a bamboo-hat-shaped pavilion called Guju Pavilion. It is a nice place to have a view of the rang upon rang of hills in the distance. By Chai Baozhong

46

47

48

46. The scene is of enchanting beauty with the white pear blossom under the bright moonlight. By Ji Zeng
47. The maple grove looks like a green islet in the distance. By Ji Zeng
48. The Club Stone in the setting sun, a scene favored by Emperor Kangxi. By Chen Baosen
49. The Club Stone, 59.42 m high, stands on the east bank of the Wulie River. Thick on top and thin at bottom, it looks like a wooden club used to beat clothes in washing, hence the name. By Chen Keyin

50

50. Putuozongchengzhimiao. By Chen Keyin

Magnificent Imperial Temples

- Outside the palace wall are a group of temples scattered in the east and north, known as the Eight Outlying Temples. Built during the 52nd year of the reign of Emperor Kangxi (1713) and the 45th year of the reign of Emperor Qianlong (1780), they look magnificent with gorgeous colors.
- That the Qing emperors launched an immense construction project of these grand temples was to show their respect to the religious beliefs of the Mongolian and Tibetan upper circles, and to strengthen the relations between the central and the local governments and consolidate the unification of the country.
- The Outlying Temples incorporates the essences of the religious architectural arts of the Han, Mongolian and Tibetan peoples. They are a rare treasure of architectural arts.

Magnificent Imperial Temples

The world-known Outlying Temples in Chengde were built during 1713 and 1780, covering a total ground of 43 ha and a construction area of 60,000 sq. m. They combine the best of the architectural arts of the Han, Mongolian and Tibetan nationalities with different styles. Each temple has its tale of history and the 12 temples record the policies toward the minority nationalities made by Emperor Kangxi and Emperor Qianlong.

51

I. Purensi: First of the Eight Outlying Temples

Purensi (Temple of Universal Love) was the earliest of the Eight Outlying Temples. It was built in the 52nd year of the reign of Emperor Kangxi (1713) when his 60th birthday was celebrated. The Mongolian nobles requested a temple be built to show their loyalty and support to the emperor and congratulations and commemorations as well. Approved by the emperor, two temples of Puren and Pushan were built on the east bank of the Wulie River. As the first imperial temple in the Mountain Resort, Purensi reflects the policies of the Qing court toward the administration over the Mongolian tribes. The relations between the Manchu and the Mongolian nobility was different from the attempts of emperors of the Han Dynasty to cement relations with rulers of minority Xiongnu, who lived in the north border area, by marrying daughters of the Han imperial family to them, nor was it similar to the terms accepted by the Song court under the duress of the Khitan who had reached the city wall of the Song. The Manchu nobility held that the Mongolian tribes would be stronger than the Great Wall as a defense in the north, and made a set of administrative measures based on this. First of all, general control over the Inner Mongolia and the league and banner system of the vassal state of Outer Mongolia was implemented. The Inner Mongolia was divided into Eight Nomadic Banners, while leagues and banners were set up on the basis of the old division of grand suzerain, marquis and small domain as practiced by the Outer Mongolia. Meanwhile, six titles of nobility would be conferred to those Mongolian feudal lords, including prince and duke. Thus, the Mongolian upper circles could have the same ranks as the Manchu nobility and get greatly satisfied both in material and in psychology. The Qing court had never ceased their relative relations with the Mongolians in the north and had tried to consolidate their political alliance through marriage relations. The building of the two temples was to further strengthen the relation with and control over the Mongolians.

51.Inside the Ciyun Puyin Dian of the Purensi are enshrined the wooden statues of Mahakasyapa, Sakyamuni and Maitreya, with simple and easy bearings. By Chen Keyin

52. Purensi, the earliest of the Eight Outlying Temples, is in typical architectural style of the Han people, with compact layout and regular square courtyard. By Chen Keyin

53.On the board inside the Ciyun Puyin Dian are inscriptions by Emperor Kangxi on the reasons for building the temple, and poems by Emperor Qianlong praising the beautiful scenery here. By Chen Keyin

52

53

54

II. Puningsi: in Han and Tibetan Styles

Puningsi (Temple of Universal Peace) is a rare temple in the country that incorporates the architectural styles of the Han and the Tibetan peoples: the front part in Han style and the rear part completely modeled on Tibetan temples. Inside the Dachengzhige, or Hall of Mahayana, is enshrined the Avalokitesvara, the Goddess of Mercy, towering 22.28 m (excluding the small Buddha of Infinite Light on top of the head). The spectacular Buddha has 1,000 arms and 1,000 eyes, and is the highest wooden Buddha statue on earth. The statue was pieced together with 120 cu. m. of pine, cypress, elm, China fir and Chinese linden and weighs 110 tons. Despite the huge image, the entire model is well-balanced with fluent clothes lines and a full-grown figure that was treasured in the Tang Dynasty. Besides, 10,090 gilded clay statues of Buddha of Infinite Life are enshrined in the niches on the walls. With large and small statues well arranged inside the hall, it is indeed a house of art treasures.

In May of the 20th year of the reign of Emperor Qianlong (1755), the Qing government suppressed a separatist rebellion of the Mongolian Zungars. In October, the emperor held a banquet for the leaders of the Eleut Mongolians, comprising four Mongolian tribes of Zungars, Derbet, Guit and Khoshod, and conferred them high ranks of nobility according to the practice of the Manchu nobles. Since they had a belief in Lamaism, Emperor Qianlong followed the suit of his grandfather, Emperor Kangxi who had Huizong Temple built in Duolun Nur to pacify the Khalkha Mongol, and had Puningsi built in the north of the resort as a kind of commemoration, which was modeled on the Samye Monastery in Shannan, Tibet. Inside the Stele Pavilion are three steles which tell how the Mongolian rebellions were put down and the reason for building the temple.

54. Puningsi, also called Temple of Giant Buddha, is a rare temple in a combined architectural style of the Han and the Tibetan peoples. The towering buildings, terraces and pagodas amidst the pines and cypresses make a pleasant scene.

By Liu Aimin

55

55. The Hall of Mahayana, also named Sanyinlou, is the main building in Puningsi, which enshrines a 1,000-arm and 1,000-eye Buddha. By Chen Baosen

56

57

56. The 1,000-arm and 1,000-eye Avalokitesvara, towering 22.28 m, is the highest wooden Buddha statue on earth. By Chen Baosen

57. A full-length picture of the 1,000-arm and 1,000-eye Avalokitesvara. By Shi Yi

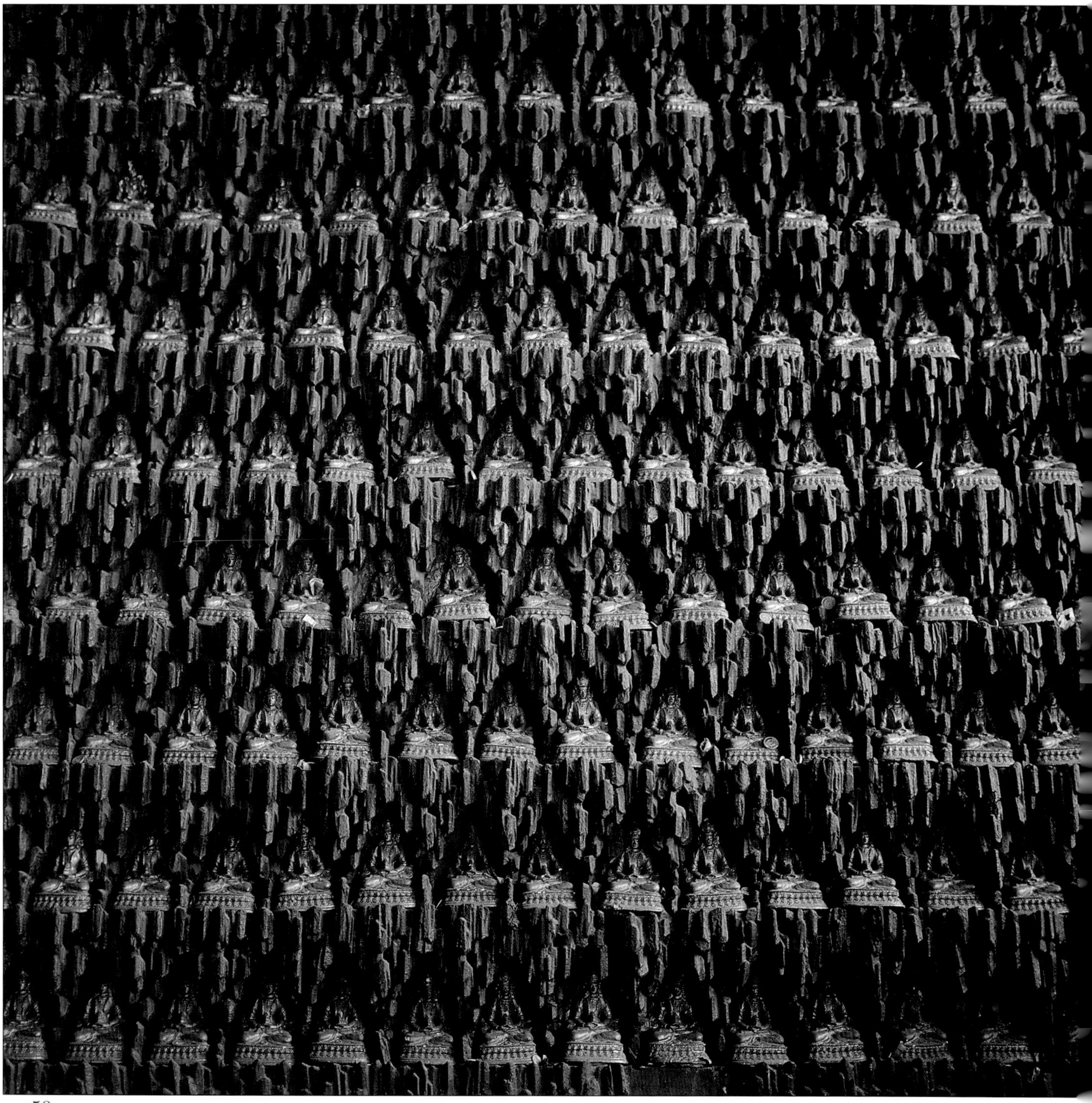

58

59

60

58. A total of 10,090 gilded clay statues of Buddha of Infinite Life are enshrined inside the Hall of Mahayana, 15 cm high each. By Du Dianwen
59. Sakyamuni, the central figure of the three gilded wooden Buddhas enshrined in the Daxiong Baodian (Precious Hall of the Great Hero). By Chen Keyin
60. The gorgeous frescoes of Tara in the Daxiong Baodian with vivid images are art treasures of Buddhist painting. By Chen Keyin

61

III. Puyousi: Institute of Buddhism

Puyousi (Temple of Universal Bless), next to the Puningsi, is the Institute of Buddhism. Built in the 25th year during the reign of Emperor Qianlong (1760), it is a temple combining the Han and Tibetan styles. Besides the hall of Buddha, it has hall of scripture and halls of studies. The temple is called "gcwa-tshang" in Tibetan language, that is, monastery. In center of the rear courtyard is a square hall of scripture, 7 bays long and 7 bays wide. The horizontal tablet says "Hall of the Wheel of the Law", with the inscription by Emperor Qianlong. A gilded copper statue of Sakyamuni is enshrined in the hall, with the inscriptions engraved on the back of the statue, recording its unusual experience. The Eleut Mongolians who believed in Lamaism built the famous Golden Top Temple by the Ili River. The Buddha statues, musical instruments used in a Buddhist mass and sacrificial utensils were worshipped by the Eleut tribes. Unfortunately, the temple was destroyed in war. Emperor Qianlong was very sad about it. He ordered the burnt scrap copper collected to mold a new gilded statue of Sakyamuni enshrined in the Hall of the Wheel of the Law inside the Puyousi for the Eleut tribal heads to pay homage when they came to have audiences with the emperor. There are halls of studies in the Puyousi: Hall of Tibetan Medicine with doctor's degree of medicine, Hall of Abacus with doctor's degree of calendar, the Esoteric Hall with doctor's degree of Esoteric Sect, and the Hall of Scripture Studies with doctor's degree of Open Schools. Puyousi not only trains lamas of its own, but also receives Mongolian lamas from other monasteries.

62

63

64

65

61. Vivid gilded clay statues of arhat can rival the Hall of Arhat in Beijing's Temple of Azure Clouds. By Liu Aimin

62-65. Lively expressions of the arhat, treasures of the Qing statue arts. By Liu Aimin

IV. Anyuanmiao: An Imitation of An Ili Temple

Anyuanmiao (Temple of Conciliating People From Afar), nicknamed Ili Temple, was built in the 29th year of the reign of Emperor Qianlong (1764) and modeled on the Guerzha Temple in Ili, Xinjiang. The architectural layout is compact with three layers of walls. The main building, Pududian (Hall of Delivering All From Torment), sits in the middle of 64 surrounding rooms on the four sides. It is the only hall in the Eight Outlying Temples in the Mountain Resort that is roofed with black glazed tiles. The Green *Tara* is enshrined in the hall, with scripture picture about the goddess on the wall. During the reign of Emperor Qianlong, few nobles of the Zungars tribe of the Eleut Mongolians launched an armed rebellion, which was against by another tribe who helped the Qing court put down the rebellion. After that, they (2,100 people) were allowed to migrate to Jehol and Anyuanmiao was built for them to worship, a show of conciliation of the central government to those from afar.

66

66. Anyuanmiao was built for the Eleut Mongolians who migrated from Ili to Jehol. By Ning Zhiming

67. The scriptural picture of the Tara in the Pududian of the Anyuanmiao. By Chen Keyin

68. The Green Tara enshrined in the Pududian is the incarnation of Goddess of Mercy in legends. By Chen Keyin

67

V. Xuguangge of Pulesi: A Round Pavilion

Pulesi (Temple of Universal Happiness), also called Round Pavilion, was built in the 31st year of the reign of Emperor Qianlong (1766). Located on a mound in the northeast of the resort, the imposing building was said to be where the lamas attained the Way. Inside the Zongyindian are enshrined three Buddhas: Sakyamuni in the center flanked by Baisajya of the Oriental Pure Land and Amitabha of the Western Paradise. Behind the Zongyindian is a square stone terrace called "Ducheng". It symbolizes the Mount Sumeru, the highest mountain where Buddhas live and the center of the Buddhist universe. The Xuguangge (Hall of Brightness) on the "Ducheng" symbolizes the center of the Mount Sumeru. Xuguangge, a cone-shaped structure with a double-eaved roof, was built after the Hall of Prayer for Good Harvests in Beijing's Temple of Heaven. On the round caisson ceiling are exquisitely painted two gilded dragons playing with a ball. In the center of the hall is a big wooden Mandala, the place for the Esoteric Sect of Buddhism to perform rites. In the Mandala are enshrined a male Buddha and a female Buddha, Bde-mchog-rdo-rje, who are in the posture of intercourse, hence, they are called Buddhas of Joy.

The name of Pulesi has an implication of "universal happiness". Taking the names of the three temples of Puning (Universal Peace), Anyuan (Conciliating People From Afar) and Pule together, they mean peace comes before conciliation, and conciliation before happiness.

69

69. Pulesi, also called Round Pavilion, has two parts: the front in Han style and the rear in Tibetan style. By Ji Zeng

70

71

70. Xuguangge in Pulesi is a cone-shaped hall with a double-eaved roof covered by yellow glazed tiles, a model on the Hall of Prayer for Good Harvests in Beijing's Temple of Heaven. By Li Wenquan

71. Two gilded dragons playing with one ball painted on the caisson ceiling of the Xuguangge. By Hou Guilan

72. The Buddhas of Joy enshrined in the big Mandala on the round marble terrace in the Xuguangge. By Chen Keyin

72

73

75

74

76

According to Buddhist sutra, the four heavenly guardians were assigned jobs by Sakyamuni to defend Buddhism from monsters.

73. The State Keeping Heavenly Guardian in the East (Dhrtarastra) with a pipa.
By Liu Aimin
74. The Sharp-Eye Heavenly Guardian in the West (Virupaksa) with a snake.
By Liu Aimin
75. The Enlargement Heavenly Guardian in the South (Virudhaka) with a sword.
By Liu Aimin
76. The Sharp-Hearing Heavenly Guardian in the North (Dhanada) with an umbrella.
By Liu Aimin

77

VI. Putuozongchengzhimiao: Lesser Potala Palace

Putuozongchengzhimiao (Temple of Potarak Doctrine) was first built in 1767. Occupying 220,000 sq. m., it is made up of 40 halls of Buddhas and rooms for monks, and is the largest of the Eight Outlying Temples. Since it was modeled on the Potala Palace in Lhasa, Tibet, it is also known as Lesser Potala Palace. The red and white terraces and the ladder-shaped windows are of dense Tibetan architectural flavor. In the 35th year of the reign of Emperor Qianlong (1770), the whole country celebrated the 60th birthday of the emperor and the following year the 80th birthday of his mother. It was a grand national event in feudal society when the birthdays of the emperor and the empress dowager came together. The celebration activities were arranged to be held in Chengde because most people assembling were Mongolians or Tibetans who believed in Lamaism. To show his respect to their religious belief and to display the national strength, Emperor Qianlong had the Lesser Potala Palace built within four years. The 43-m-high Dahongtai (Great Red Terrace) has six glazed niches in the center where Buddhas of Infinite Life were enshrined. The lucky number "six" symbolized the 60th birthday of the emperor. As the temple was to be completed, a great event happened that shook the world. The Torguts, one of the four Eleut Mongolian tribes, left the Volga grasslands and returned to the embrace of the motherland.

In late the Ming Dynasty and early the Qing Dynasty, the leaders of the nomadic Torguts in the vast region to the northwest of Tacheng, Xinjiang, didn't get along well with

78

the Zungars in the Ili River Valley, and led their tribe to migrate to the Volga Valley. They broke through brambles and thorns, built yurts, and finally settled on the desolated banks of the Volga River. Later, the tsarist Russia expanded to the region and attacked the Torguts who were forced to sign treaties of humiliation. The Russians even forced the Torguts to accept the baptism of the Orthodox Eastern Church and send their leader's son to Petrograd as a hostage. The Torguts could no longer endure the exorbitant taxes and levies and national discrimination and revolted in winter of 1770. After a long, arduous journey, they finally returned to the motherland. Wobashi, head of the Torguts, paid an audience to the emperor in the Mountain Resort along with other minority leaders, when there was an exciting scene of national unification.

77. Emperor Qianlong received the leaders of the Torguts, who had just returned to the homeland, in the Mulan Imperial Hunting Ground. Courtesy of Chen Keyin
78. Putuozongchengzhimiao was ordered built within four years by Emperor Qianlong to show the respect to the religious belief of the Mongolians and the Tibetans and demonstrate the national strength. By Chen Keyin

80

79. In the middle of the walls on the Dahongtai are six niches with six glazed Buddhas of Infinite Life enshrined. By Ji Zeng
80. Laksmi enshrined in the Trilokya Pavilion is a heavenly guardian of Buddhism. By Liu Aimin

81

82

81.Dahongtai, the main building of the Putuozongchengzhimiao, has various pavilions, towers, halls and chambers in the Han style besides Tibetan red and white terraces. By Li Wenquan

82. Standing on the White Terrace are five lamaseries of black, white, yellow, green and red colors from east to west, each symbolizing a sect of Buddhism. By Ji Jiuli

83

84

83. Inside the Wanfa Guiyi Dian is a board with the inscription of "Wanyuan Puying"by Emperor Qianlong, saying all predestined relationships could be realized here. By Chen Keyin

84.Diversified architectural styles in the Putuozongchengzhimiao. By Ji Zeng

85

VII. Shuxiangsi: Ancestral Temple of Emperor Qianlong

The 26th year of the reign of Emperor Qianlong happened to be the 70th birthday of the empress dowager. The emperor accompanied his mother to hold a Buddhist service in Mount Wutai in Shanxi Province. The mountain is said to be the place where Manjusri reveals himself, therefore, the Temple of Manjusri was built and the portraits of him enshrined. The empress dowager memorized the portrait and returned to the capital. To fulfill the cherished desire of her, the emperor had Baoxiangsi (Temple of Treasure Portrait) built in the Fragrant Hills in Beijing and Shuxiangsi (Temple of Manjusri) in Chengde.

Huichengdian, the main hall, enshrines three Bodhisattvas: Manjusri in the center, Avalokitesvara on his right and Samantabhadra on his left. The word Manjusri sounds familiar to Manchu, therefore, the Dalai Lama addressed Emperor Qianlong respectfully as Manjusri Emperor. The emperor thus was regarded the reincarnation of the Manjusri. The Shuxiangsi, which enshrines the Manjusri, also holds up Emperor Qianlong as the reincarnation of the Buddha, and scriptures written in Manchu language are consecrated in the temple. Besides, the temple is in the charge of Manchu lamas and has 60 Manchu lamas living in it to study and chant those scriptures, therefore it is considered as the ancestral temple of the Manchu people and Emperor Qianlong.

Shuxiangsi has solemn halls and lovely rockeries and gardens as well. The whole temple is buried amidst old pines and cypresses and the halls are built among rockeries, thus incorporating religious connotation with gardening art and setting a good example for architectural design.

85. Shuxiangsi blends religious site with unique gardening arts, setting a model for temple building. By Liu Aimin

86. As the name suggests, Shuxiangsi enshrines Manjusri, its main Buddha, in the middle of the three Buddhas. By Chen Keyin

86

87

VIII. Xumifushouzhimiao: An Imitation of Zhaxilhunbu Monastery

The date of August 13 in the 45th year of Emperor Qianlong's reign (1780) was the 70th birthday of the emperor. Among those Mongolian tribal heads, high officials and foreign envoys coming to offer their congratulations to the emperor, the Sixth Panchen Lama was quite conspicuous who made a long journey to the Mountain Resort. The emperor showed special concern to his visit. He followed the suit of his great-grandfather, Emperor Shunzhi who had Xihuangsi Temple built in Beijing when he received the Fifth Dalai Lama, and ordered Xumifushouzhimiao (Temple of Sumeru Happiness and Longevity) completed within two years. The temple was an imitation of the Zhaxilhunbu Monastery in Tibet, where the Panchen Lama lived. "Xumifushouzhimiao" is the transliteration of the Tibetan "Zhaxilhunbu Monastery" in Chinese. The temple is also called the Temporary Residence of the Panchen Lama in Chengde.

The Miaogao Zhuangyan Dian enshrines Tsongkhapa, the founder of the Yellow Sect of Lamaism. It was in this hall that Emperor Qianlong listened to the Sixth Panchen Lama expounding the texts of Buddhism and accepted abhiseca, and that Panchen Lama offered his congratulations on the occasion of the emperor's birthday.

The presentation of Tibetan religious leaders before the emperor began with the Fifth Dalai Lama. That the Sixth Panchen Lama visited Chengde and Beijing to have audiences with Emperor Qianlong was not called in by the court, but of his free will. To the emperor, that the Sixth Panchen Lama covered a long journey to congratulate on his 70th birthday was a symbol of the auspiciousness and prosperity of the country, and he would spare no effort to make detailed reception plans for Panchen. The munificent imperial favors and gorgeous rewards to the Panchen Lama were all out of the aim of consolidating the political power of the Qing court. Under such a special circumstance, the visit of the Sixth Panchen Lama helped strengthen the relations between the Tibetan local government and the central government, and solidify the development of a united multi-nationality country.

87. Xumifushouzhimiao, modeled on Zhaxilhunbu Monastery in Xigaze, Tibet, blends Han and Tibetan architectural arts. By Zhou Yi

91

88. The 7-story Wanshouta (Pagoda of Longevity) sits on a mountain north of the Xumifishouzhimiao, covered with green glazed bricks and exquisite niches. By Li Wenquan
89. Golden dragons playing with a ball on the glazed memorial archway. By Ji Zeng
90. The statue of Tsongkhapa, founder of the Yellow Sect, enshrined in the Miaogao Zhuangyan Dian. By Liu Aimin
91. The glazed memorial archway in front of the Great Red Terrace looks like the main gate to the terrace. A pair of marble elephants on both sides symbolize the huge power of Buddhism. By Liu Aimin

88

89

90

92

92. The magnificent Xumifishouzhimiao and other temples set off by the rosy clouds and the setting sun.
By Yang Haitao

94

93

95

96

97

93. Miaogao Zhuangyan Dian, where the Sixth Panchen Lama expounded the texts of Buddhism, glitters in the sun with a pointed end and a double-eaved roof covered with fishscaled glazed tiles.
By Chen Baosen
94. The four roof ridges of Miaogao Zhuangyan Dian each has two gilded copper dragons.
By Liu Aimin
95. The deer ornament on the roof ridge of the turret. By Min Ren
96. The peacock ornament on the roof ridge of theturret. By Min Ren
97. Tibetan color paintings. By Min Ren

98

98. Bronze 11-faced Avalokitesvara. By Hou Guilan

Rare Treasures in the Mountain Resort and Outlying Temples

- The rare treasures collected in the Mountain Resort and Outlying Temples are an important component of the place.
- The Nanshufang and the Zaobanchu used to be special organs designing and manufacturing arts and crafts for the emperor. Workshops in other parts of the country produced exquisite handicrafts and daily necessities for the court.
- During the stay of Emperor Kangxi and Emperor Qianlong in the Mountain Resort, huge stocks of living materials and gifts were prepared for banquets and rewards and daily use of the emperor.
- A large number of rare art treasures of Lamaism are collected in the Outlying Temples such as statues of Buddhas, sacrificial utensils and musical instruments used in a Buddhist mass. Many statues have marvelous images and vivid expressions with extraordinary splendor.

Rare Treasures in the Mountain Resort and Outlying Temples

Besides royal garden, magnificent temples and rich historical connotation, the Mountain Resort has a great many rare cultural relics, which add luster to the place.

The palace relics made during the reign of Emperor Kangxi and Emperor Qianlong represent the highest level of art in the Qing Dynasty. The Nanshufang and the Zaobanchu used to be special organs designing and manufacturing arts and crafts for the emperor. Workshops in other parts of the country produced exquisite handicrafts and daily necessities for the court, for instance, the porcelain produced in Jingdezhen, the brocade made in Jiangning, the embroidery in Suzhou, the clocks and watches in Guangzhou, the enamel in Beijing and the stone carvings in Quyang.

Emperor Kangxi and Emperor Qianlong spent half of the year in the Mountain Resort. Enormous materials and gifts were needed for the daily life, banquets and rewards, consequently, a great number of various kinds of *ruyi*, snuff bottles, porcelain, silk, clocks and watches, clothes and accessories, and other jewelry were prepared in the resort. In addition, the halls, chambers and towers of the emperor and the empress were furnished with various red sandalwood furniture, porcelain made by official kilns, lacquer-wares, potted landscapes, hanging panels, Western clocks and watches, brocade appliances for chairs, etc. All these are rare art treasures.

Since the Qing court had esteem for Lamaism, the Outlying Temples are also a place storing lots of precious work of art of Lamaism, such as statues of Buddhas, sacrificial utensils and musical instruments used in a Buddhist mass. These divine utensils made by the official departments and others respectfully presented by the Mongolian and Tibetan religious leaders or heads of the ethnic groups are all gems of the Buddhist art. Besides gilded bronze and gilded wooden qualities, the statues are made of gold, silver, jade, marble, porcelain and brocade. They blend the elements of the Han, Tibetan and Nepalese peoples and exhibit the characteristics and level of the Buddhist art of the Outlying Temples.

99. Gilded bronze Laksmi. By Liu Aimin
100. Bronze Dakini of Wisdom. By Hou Guilan
101. Buddha's warrior attendant. By Hou Guilan
102. Gilded bronze Yamantaka warrior attendant. By Hou Guilan
103. Gilded bronze Bde-mchog-rdo-rje. By Hou Guilan
104. Four-armed guardian deity. By Liu Aimin

99

100

101

102

103

104

105

106

107

105. Jade Buddha of Infinite Life. By Liu Aimin
106. Gilded bronze Buddha of Infinite Life. By Hou Guilan
107. Turquoise Buddha with gold tracing. By Hou Guilan
108. Manjusri riding a lion. By Hou Guilan
109. Gilded bronze Bodhisattva. By Hou Guilan

108

109

110

111

112

110. Gilded bronze Buddhist tree. By Hou Guilan
111. Gold lacquer wood carving double-layer niche. By Hou Guilan
112. Bronze enamel bottle-gourd-shaped niche. By Chen Keyin
113. Gilded bronze Laksmi. By Hou Guilan
114. Bronze lion-head Mother of Buddha. By Hou Guilan

113

114

119

120

119. Golden white birches look even more captivating under the setting sun.
By Chen Baosen
120. Gorgeous forest in autumn.
By Zhang Liang
121. Rays of sunlight shining through the thin clouds, a charming scene at dusk.
By Zhu Enguang
122. Saihanba pasture land with plenty of water and lush grass.
By Li Shoutong
123. White yurts dotted on the carpet of green grass. By Zhang Liang

121

122

123

By Ji Weihua

Planning Staff Chen Yong
Chief Editor Ru Suichu
Editor of the volume Zhou Yi
Text Du Jiang
English Translation Han Qingyue
Layout Zhou Yi
Technical Editor WangTao

World Cultural and Natural Heritage
(China Volume)

The Mountain Resort and Outlying Temples

Compiled by: State Cultural Relics Bureau of the People's Republic of China and Beijing Jingxin Cultural Development Co., Ltd.
(8 Shangdi Sijie, Haidian District, Beijing 100085)
Published by: China Pictorial Publishing House
(33 West Chegongzhuang Road, Haidian District, Beijing 100044)
Distributed abroad by: China International Book Trading Corp.
(35 West Chegongzhuang Road, Haidian District, Beijing 100044)
Printing: Shenzhen Sanwang Printing & Packing Co.,Ltd.
Format and Printed Sheet: 6 printed sheets in 16 mo
Impression: First impression of the first edition in May 1999
Book No.: ISBN 7 - 80024 - 517 - 9
Price: Clothbound Edition ¥ 138
Paperbound Edition ¥ 108